HOW MUCH FUN IT WOULD BE TO BE A WILD ANIMAL FROM A TO Z

Written by Mike Messeroff
Illustrated by Hannah Rose Chavez

How Much Fun It Would Be To Be A Wild Animal From A To Z

Published by Happy As Dog LLC

Written by Mike Messeroff
Illustrated by Hannah R. Chavez
Cover design and illustration by Hannah R. Chavez
Book design by Hannah R. Chavez

Names: Messeroff, Mike, author. | Chavez, Hannah Rose, illustrator.

Title: How much fun would it be to be a wild animal from A to Z / written by Mike Messeroff ; illustrated by Hannah Rose Chavez.
Description: Breckenridge, CO: Happy As Dog LLC, 2020. | Summary: Wild, rare, exotic, and endangered animals of the world. This book features over 25 beautiful illustrations and rhyming poems to educate, entertain, and energize minds with wild animals like the Axolotl, Capybara, and the Lynx!
Identifiers: LCCN: 2020908051 | ISBN: 978-1-7343253-4-8 (Hardcover) | 978-1-7343253-2-4 (pbk.) | 978-1-7343253-3-1 (ebook) | 978-1-7343253-5-5 (coloring book)
Subjects: LCSH Animals--Juvenile literature. | English language--Alphabet--Juvenile literature. | Zoology--Juvenile literature. | CYAC Animals. | English language--Alphabet. | Zoology. | BISAC JUVENILE NONFICTION / Animals / General | JUVENILE NONFICTION / Concepts / Alphabet
Classification: LCC QL49 .M56 How 2020 | DDC 590--dc23

BULK ORDERS: We are happy to offer special terms for schools, companies, professional groups, clubs, and other organizations when ordering quantities of this title. For information, please email hi@happyasdog.com.

This book is printed in the United States of America.
Created with love in Breckenridge, CO and New York, NY.

Dedication

This book about animals is dedicated to every human...
Just as each animal has its own species, we too are one race. Thank you for taking care of our home, for taking care of each other, and for respecting every creature who also calls this indescribably gorgeous planet their home. We are always, and all, in this together.

And to the illustrator of this book, Hannah.
We created this book in one month, and you turned around twenty-nine illustrations in twenty-nine days! Thank you so much for sharing your amazing talents as we continue having fun and creating together!

As I was laying in bed,

a funny thought came to my head...

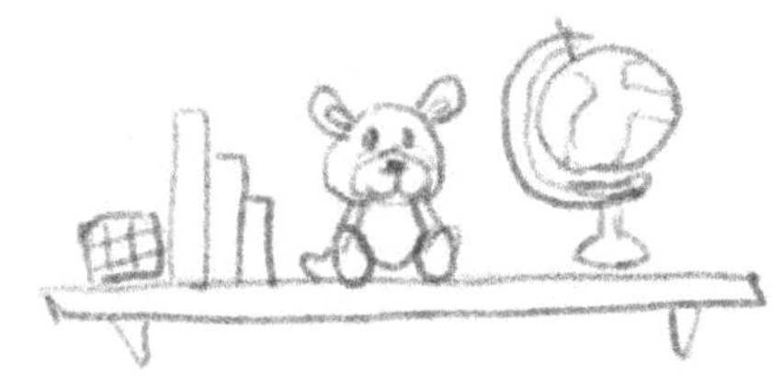

How much fun it could be,

to be something *other* than me!

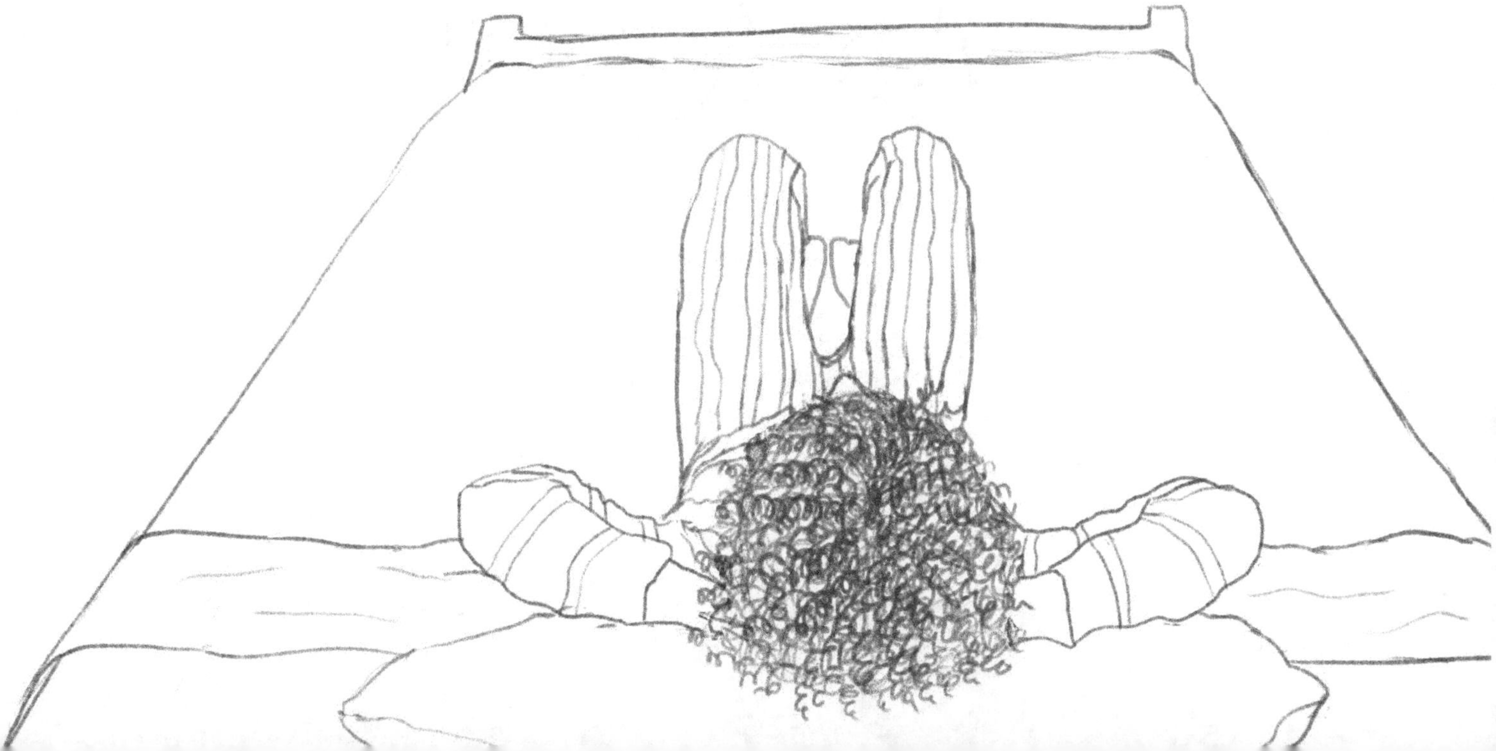

How much fun it would be,
if instead of me, I could be...

An Axolotl

(ax-uh-lot-uhl)

Underwater is where I live, like a message in a bottle,
and I swim around and smile all day as an Axolotl.
I come from one lake in Mexico, and if I lose a limb it will grow back quick,
and my beautiful gills extend out of my head...it's my stylish breathing trick.

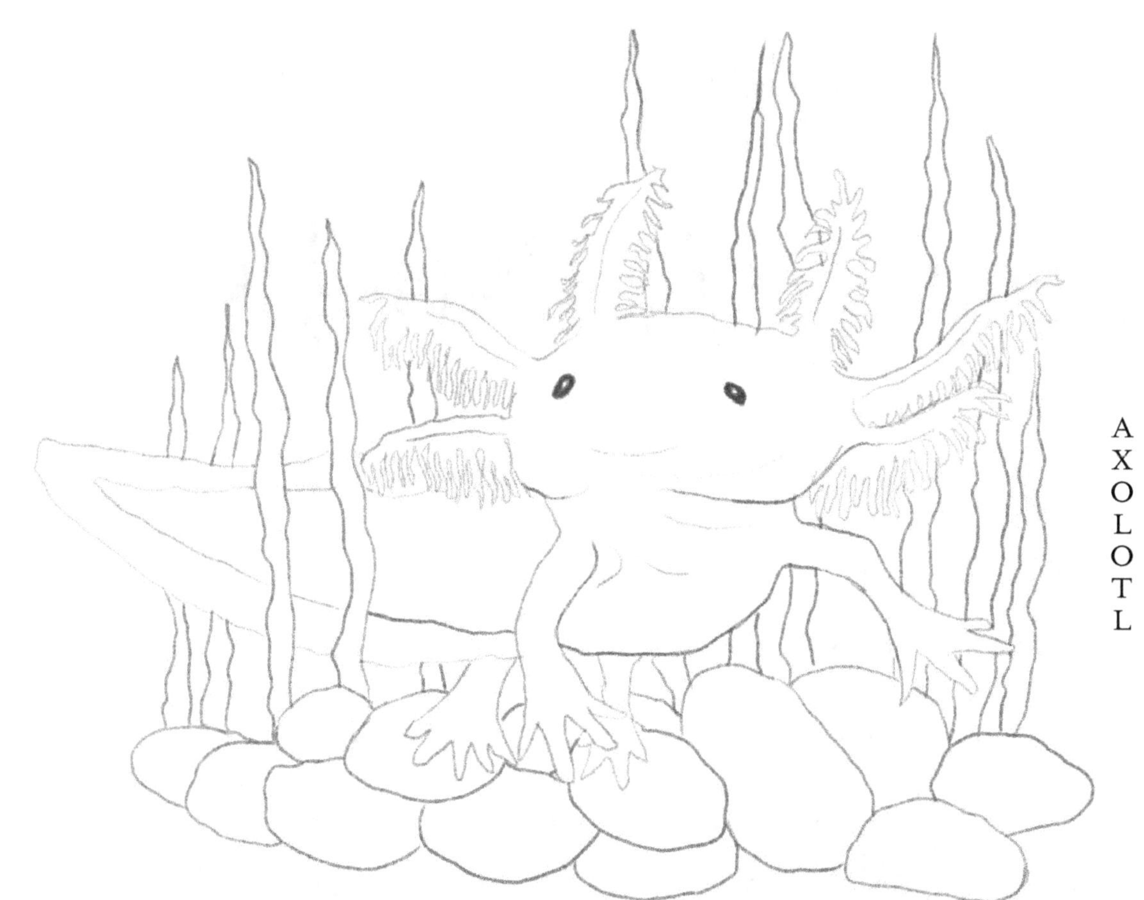

How much fun it would be,
if instead of me, I could be...

A Bonobo

(buh-no-bo)

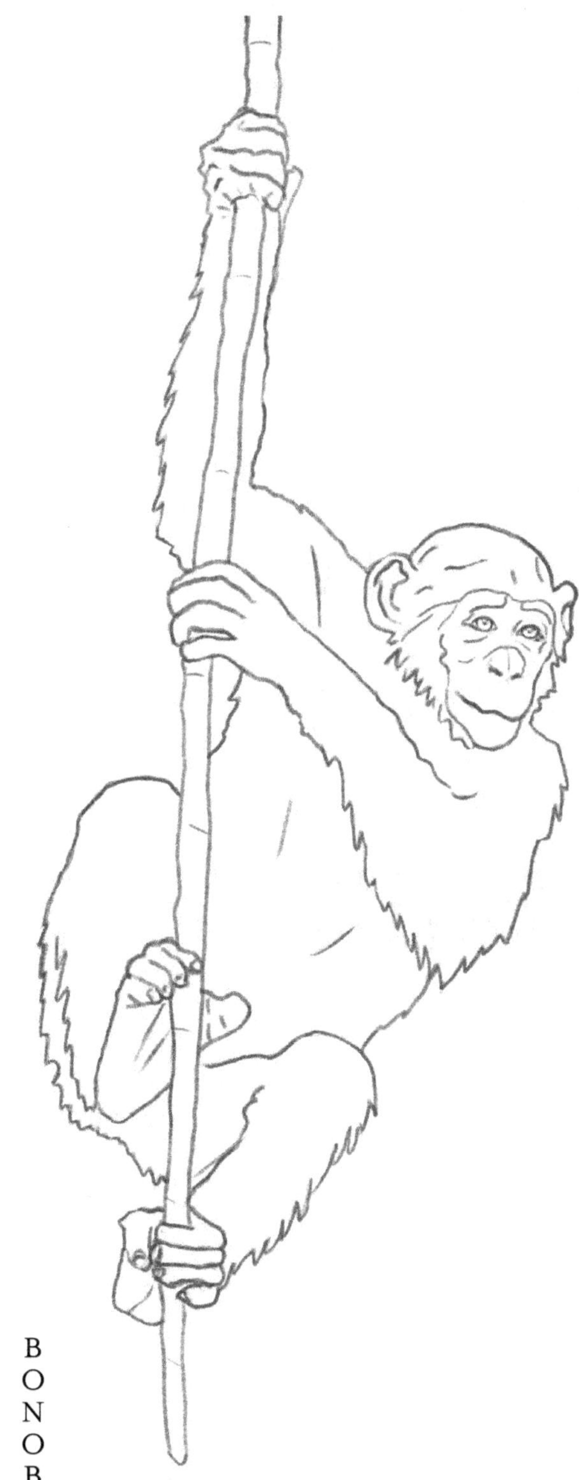

As a Bonobo, I'm a lover, not a fighter,

and life is such a blast.

I live in the Congo, the African jungle,

and I climb and swing so fast.

I'm the closest relative to humans,

along with my cousins the Chimpanzees,

and I'm also caring and kind...

and love to play in the trees!

BONOBO

How much fun it would be,
if instead of me, I could be...

A Capybara

(cap-ee-bar-ah)

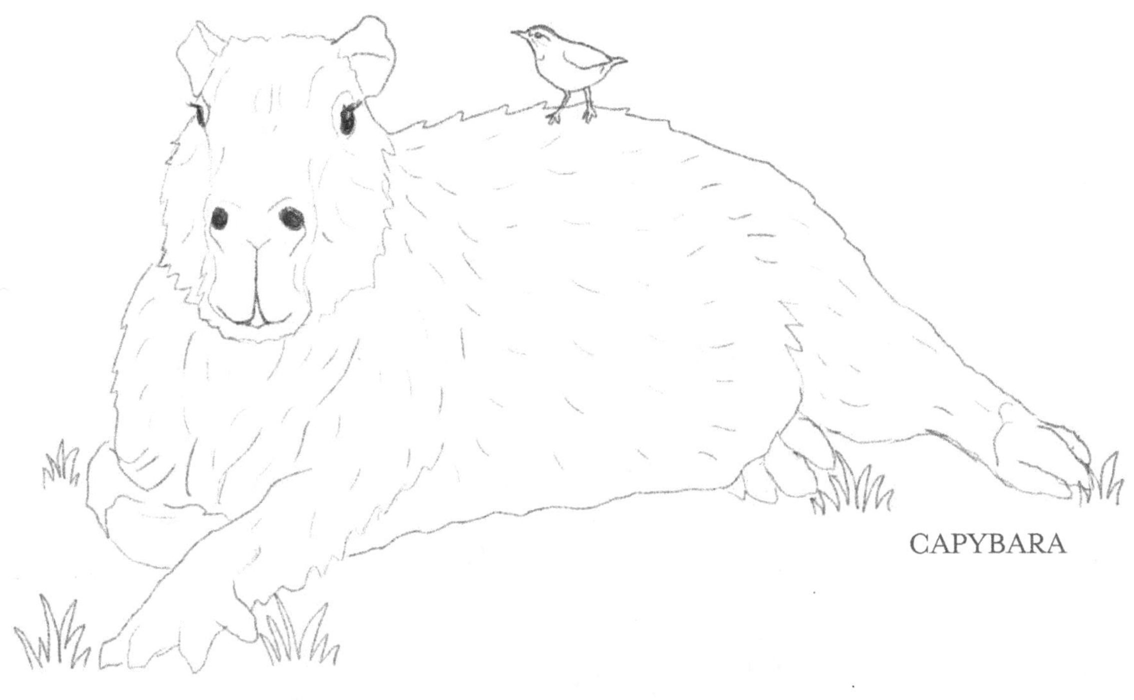

CAPYBARA

I'm similar to a guinea pig, but I weigh a hundred pounds!
As one of the friendliest animals in the world, joyfulness abounds.
I'm an amazing swimmer with the help of my webbed-feet, no doubt,
Sometimes I even sleep in the water, with just my nose sticking out.

How much fun it would be,
if instead of me, I could be...

A Dugong

(doo-gong)

As a marine mammal, I live in the ocean, near the shallow coast.

While some call me the "Sea Cow," it's not the nickname I like the most.

At 10 feet long and 650 pounds, I get it,

but I prefer "Lady of the Sea".

Old sailors called me that...

they thought I was a mermaid

when they caught a glimpse of me.

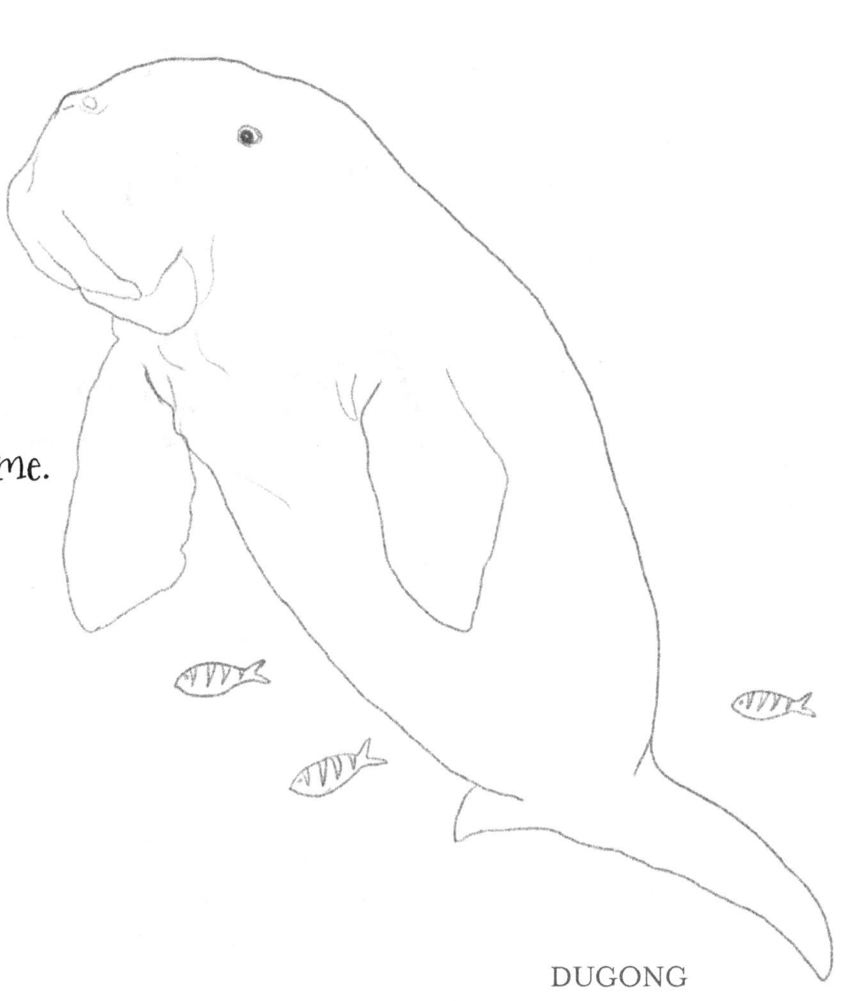

DUGONG

How much fun it would be,
if instead of me, I could be...

An Echidna

(ah-kid-na)

I roam Australia and New Guinea alone...I like my solitude,
and my long nose has special sensors to help me find my food.
The platypus and I are the only egg-laying, mammal creatures,
and I protect myself with sharp spines, they are my great defensive features!

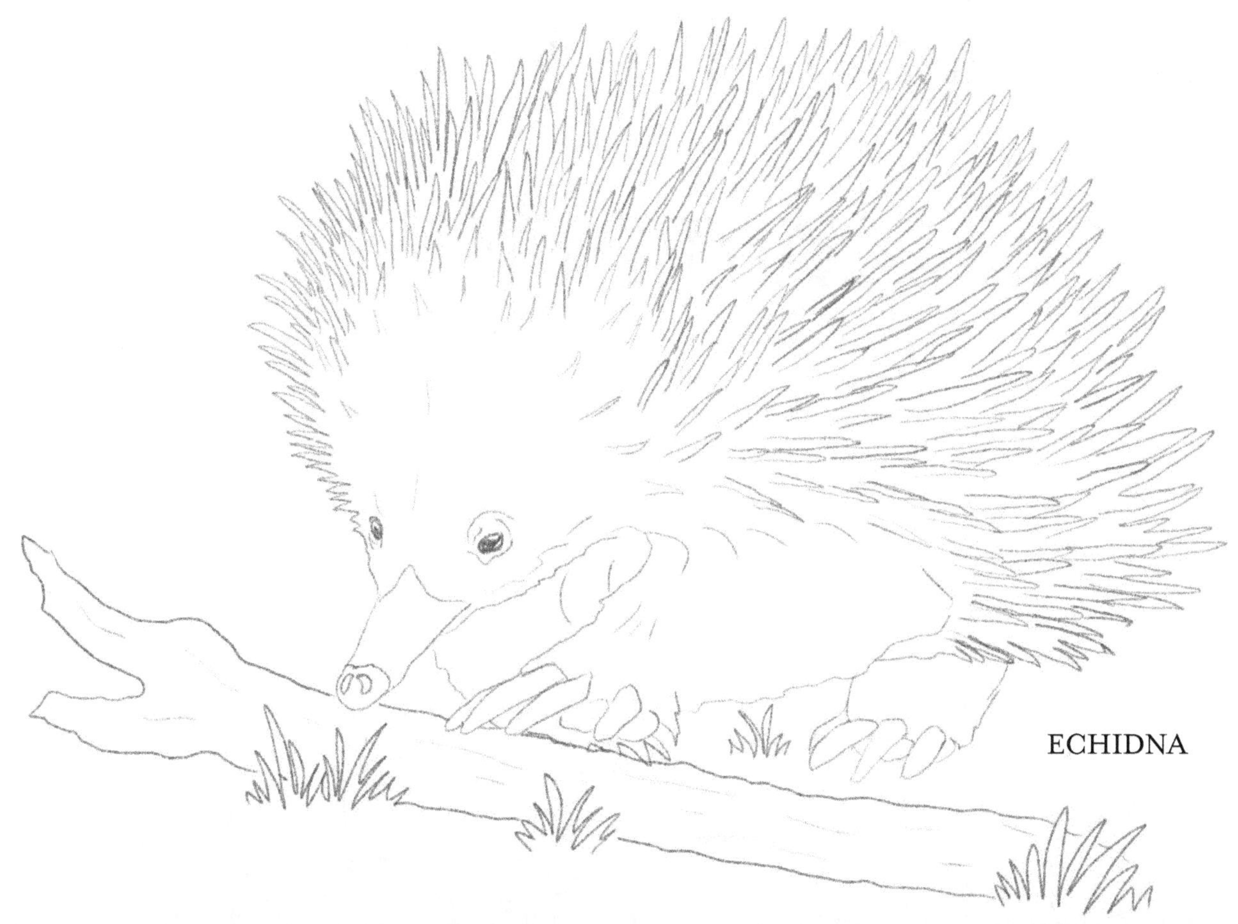

ECHIDNA

How much fun it would be,
if instead of me, I could be...

A Fossa

(foss-ah)

F O S S A

Like a cougar, I'm agile, and like a mongoose, I'm fast,
and if I race you up a tree,
you can be sure I won't come in last.
My long tail helps me balance,
and I use the trees as my playground in the sky.
My home is the island of Madagascar,
and I love to jump so high!

How much fun it would be,
if instead of me, I could be...

A Guanaco

(gwah-nock-oh)

Up in the mountains of South America,

I'm a comfortably-covered mammal.

I'm wrapped in soft wool, like cashmere,

and related to the llama, alpaca, and camel.

I live together with my family,

and I can race with great power.

Usually, though, I just roam...

but I can run 35 miles per hour!

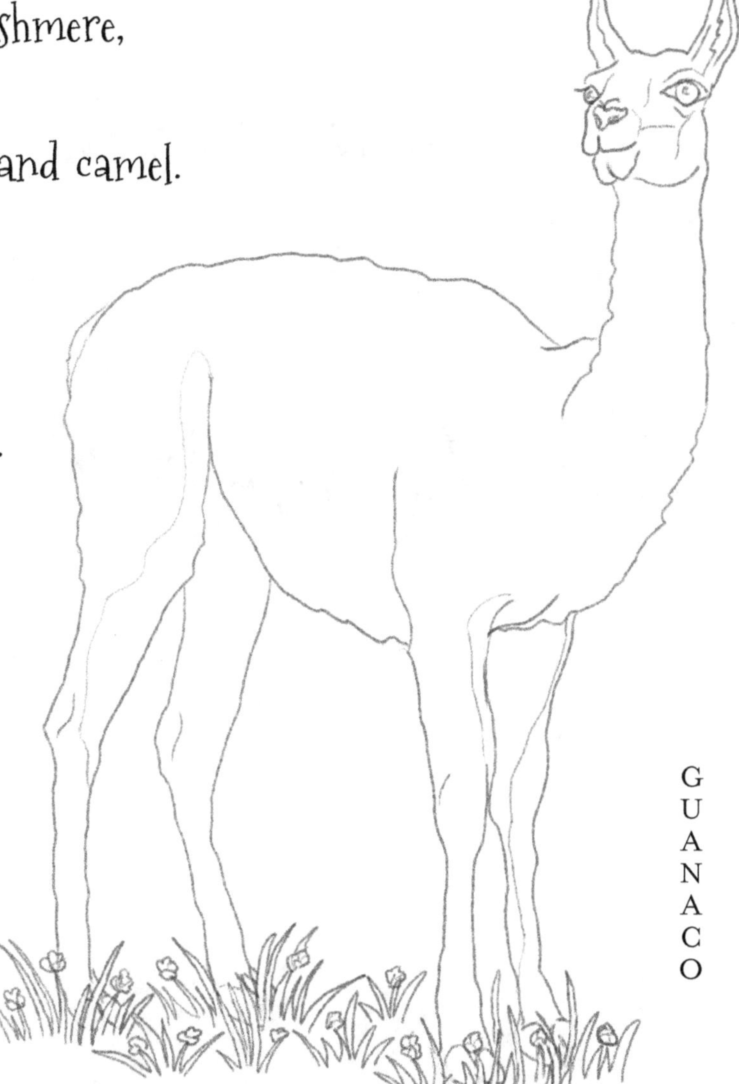

How much fun it would be,
if instead of me, I could be...

A Helmetshrike

(hel-met-shrike)

I'm a songbird and I'm quite noisy,
despite my petite size.
I live in Africa and I'm sociable,
with sunflowers around my eyes.
I have a beautiful head ornament,
it's how I got my name.
With a permanent helmet on my head,
it's my claim to fame.

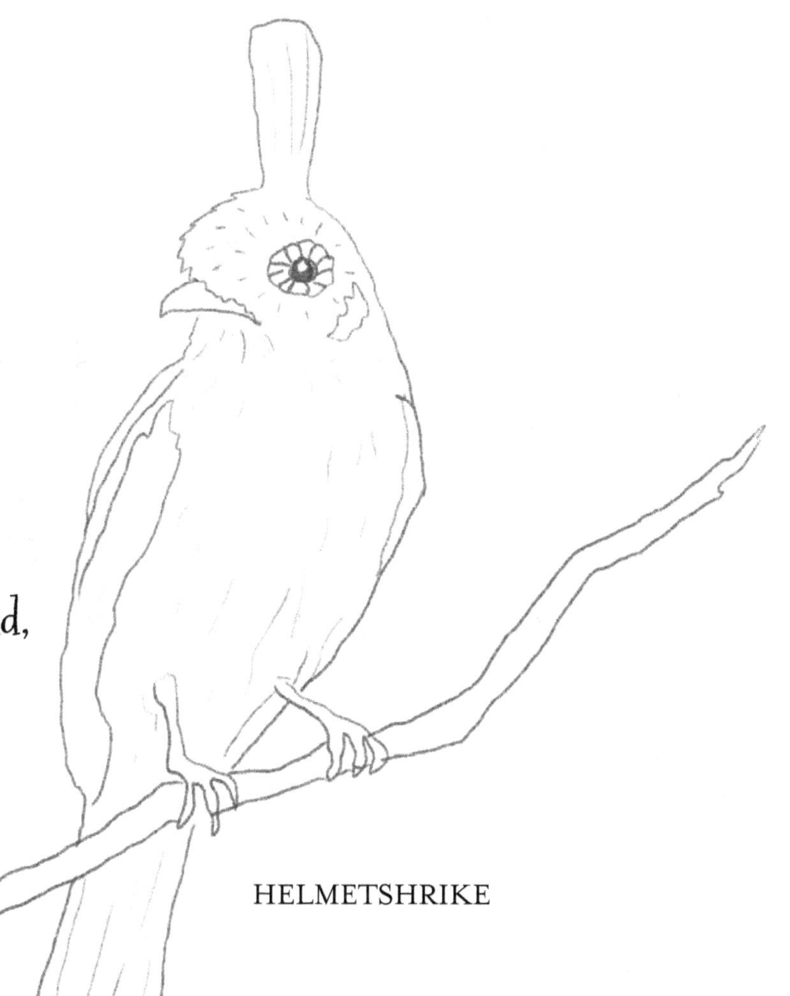

HELMETSHRIKE

How much fun it would be,
if instead of me, I could be...

An Ibex

(eye-bex)

I'm a magnificent mountain goat,
with horns so long and curvy,
and I maneuver up and down mountains with ease,
no matter how steep or how swervy.
I come from Africa, Asia, and Europe,
and I'm skilled at jumping and climbing.
I navigate mountains with balance and grace,
as well as impeccable timing.

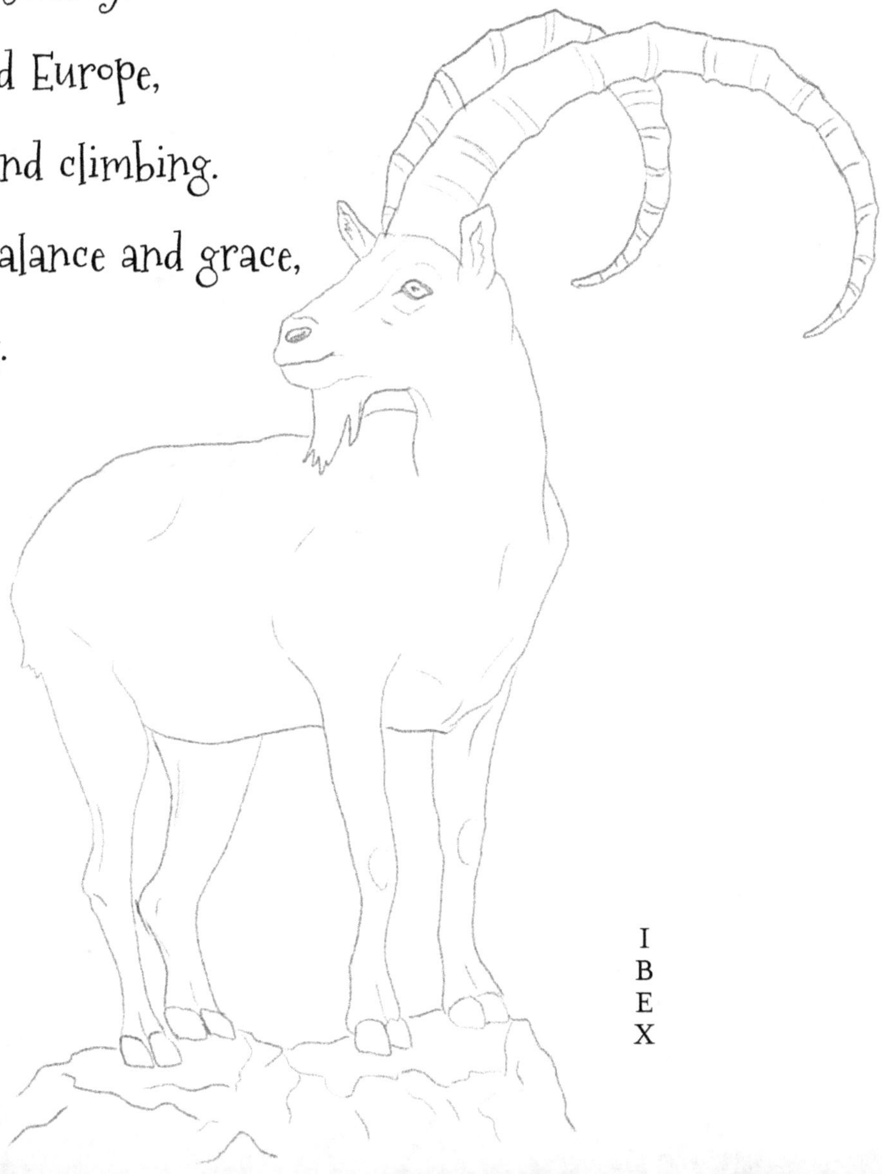

I
B
E
X

How much fun it would be,
if instead of me, I could be...

A Jacana

(juh-cah-na)

I'm a tropical and unique bird...I have a trick that's hard to beat.

I can *almost* walk on water with long toes on my feet.

Just find me a shallow lake, filled with lily pads to the brim,

and I'll be a happy Jacana, as I walk, fly and swim!

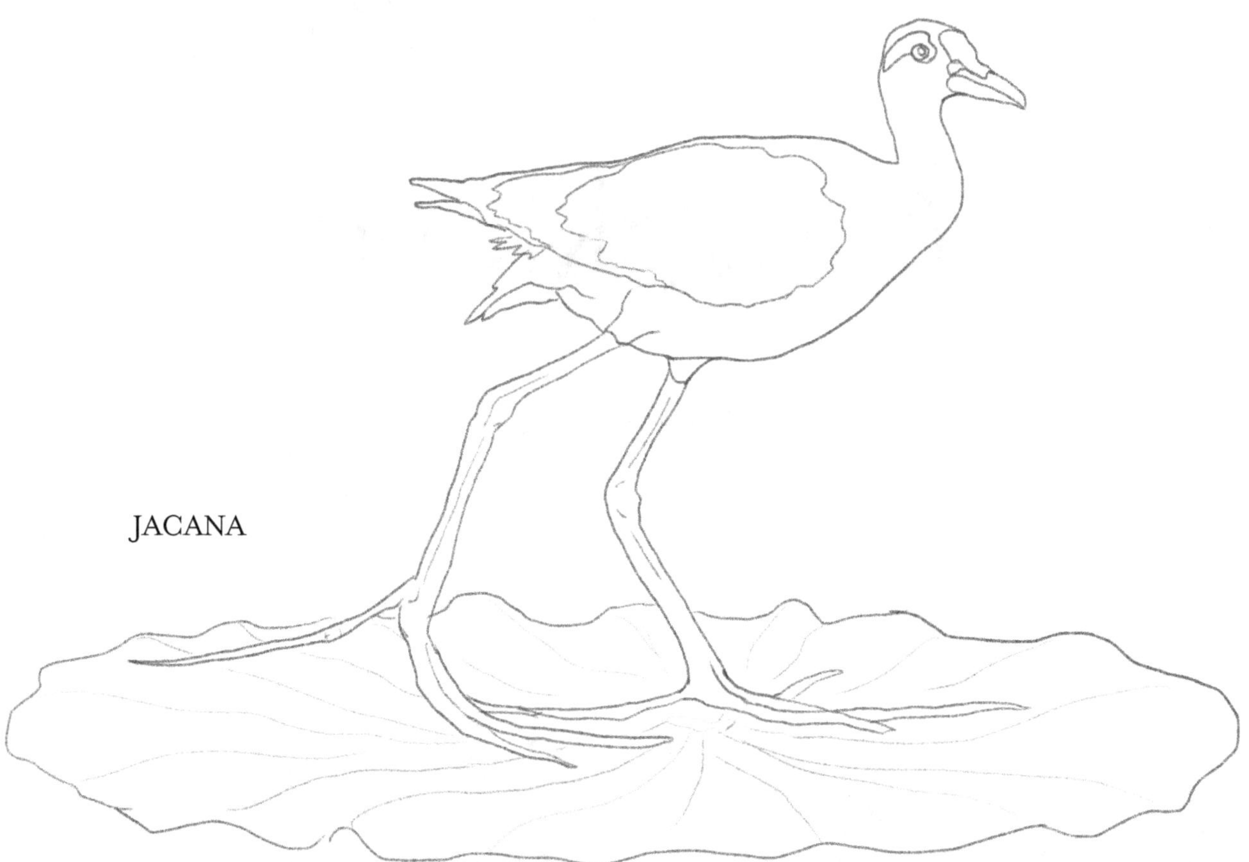

JACANA

How much fun it would be,
if instead of me, I could be...

A Kinkajou

(kink-ah-joo)

KINKAJOU

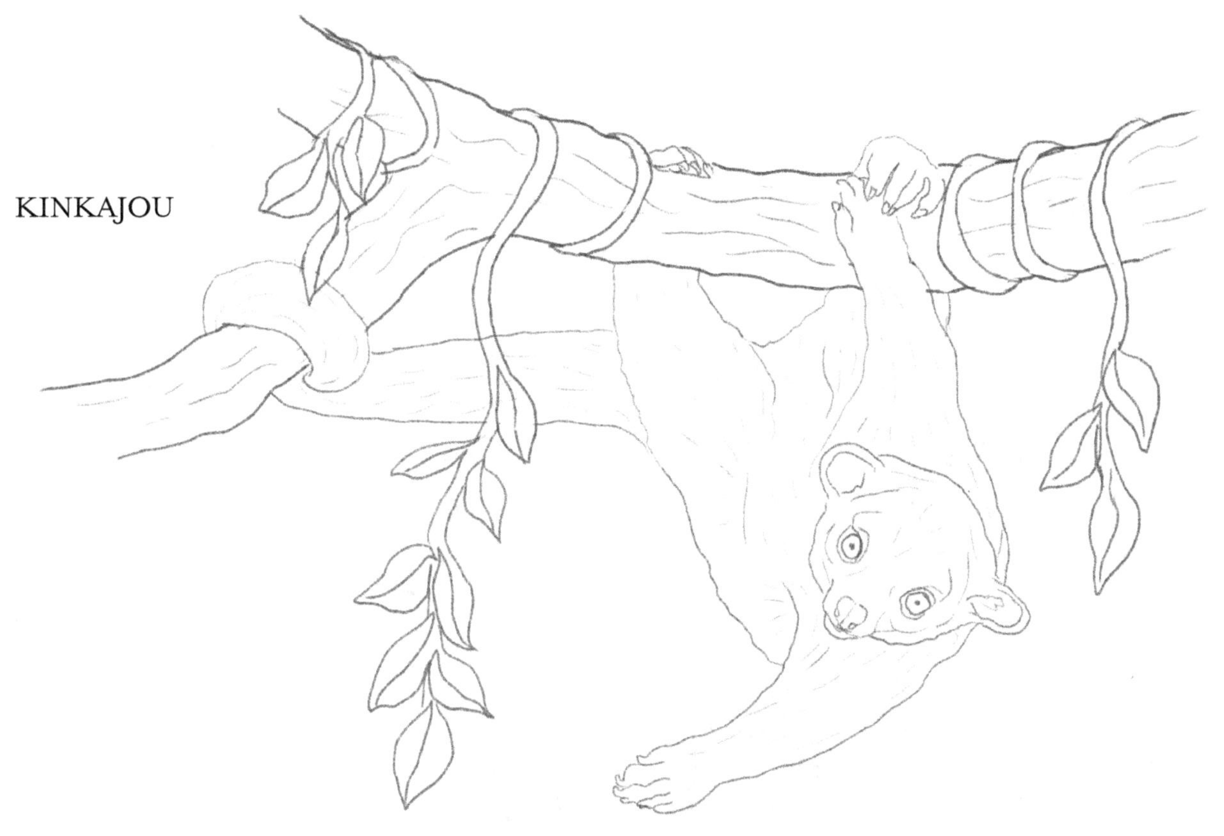

I have a prehensile tail, and it grips like a fifth arm.
With a diet of mostly fruit, I'm not causing any harm.
In the tropical rainforests, I live an arboreal life with ease,
because, although I can't fly, my life exists in the trees!

How much fun it would be,
if instead of me, I could be...

A Lynx

(links)

I trek across high altitude forests, and my skills are diverse.

I can jump, climb, swim, and run, with big paws that help me traverse.

I'm a cool and confident cat,

with tufts of black hair on each ear,

and as a mystical, stealthy Lynx,

my hearing is crystal clear.

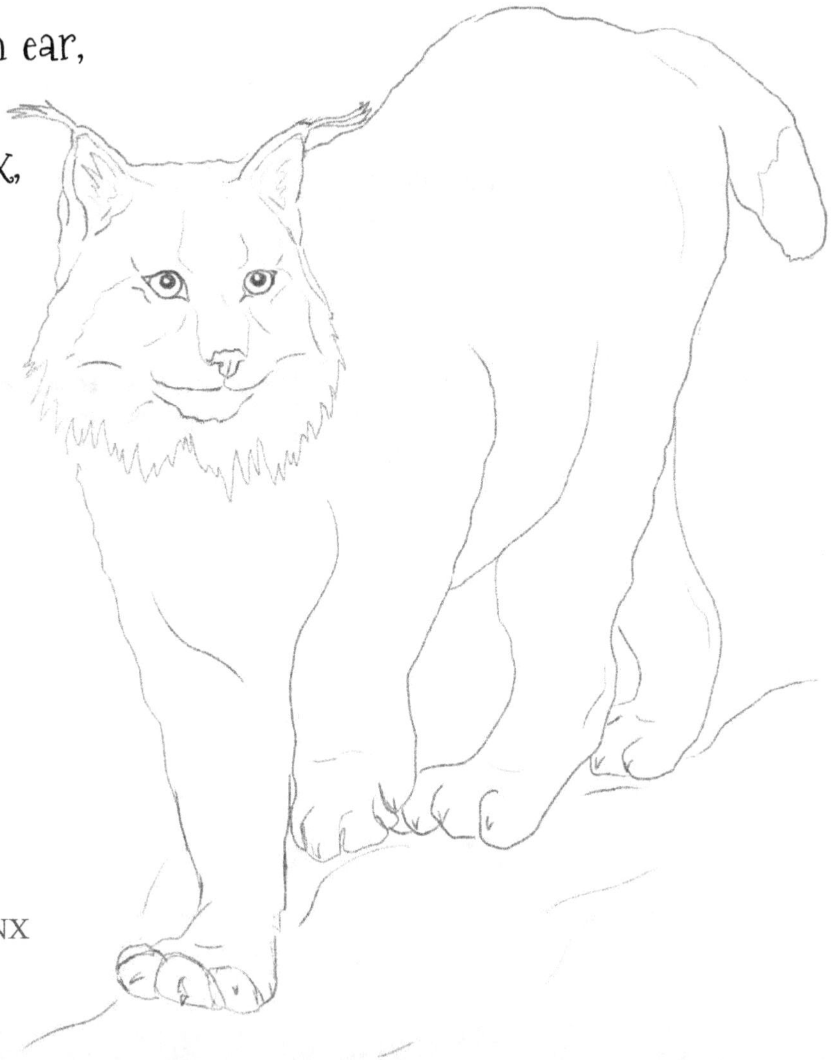

LYNX

How much fun it would be,
if instead of me, I could be...

A Marmoset

(marm-uh-set)

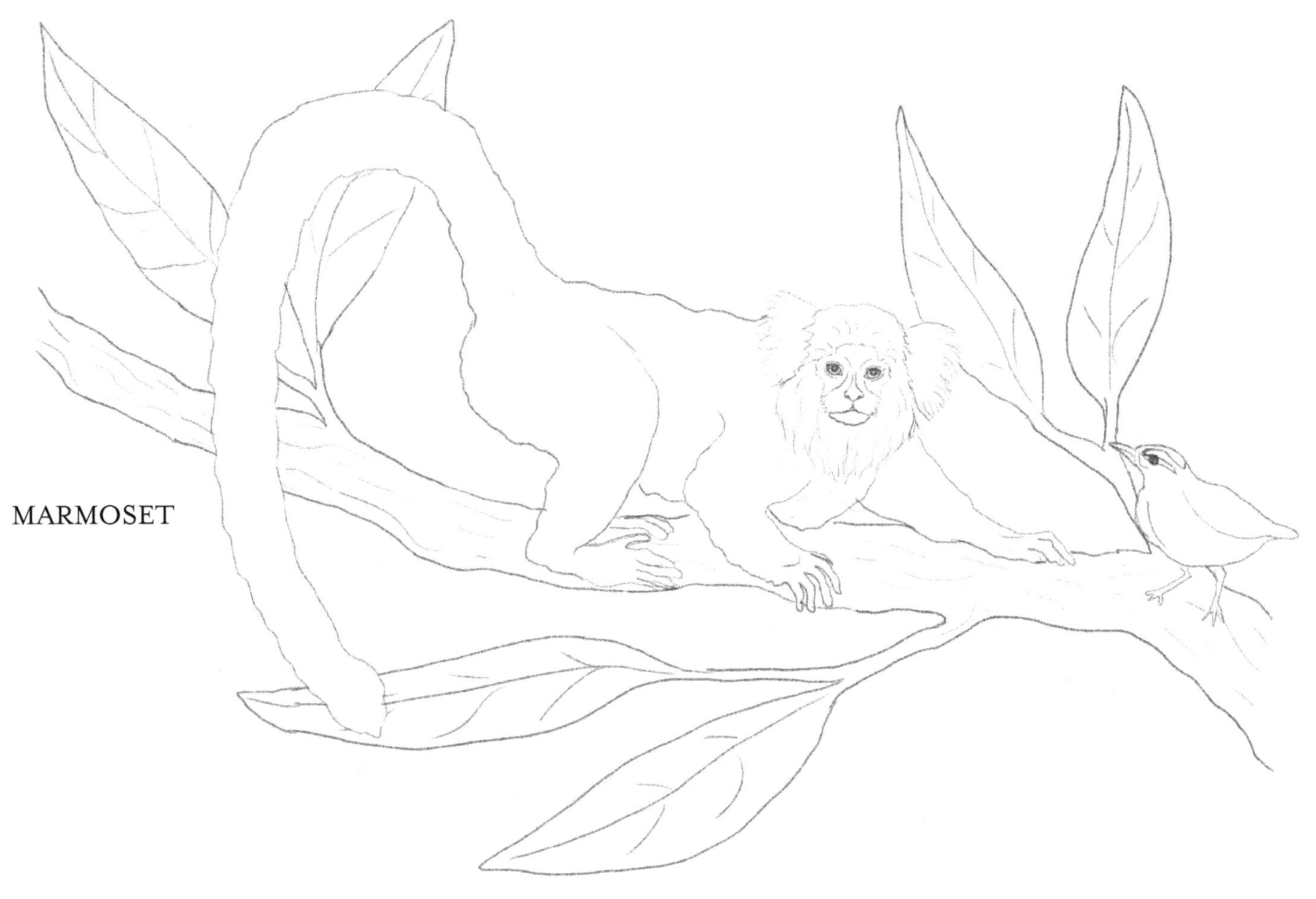

In the jungles of South America, I live with my family.

I enjoy an active and social life, high in the treetop canopy.

I'm called the "Finger Monkey", and at 8 inches long you can see why.

With a long tail and special claws, up in the trees I can almost fly.

How much fun it would be,
if instead of me, I could be...

A Nabarlek

(nah-burr-leck)

From Northern Australia, I'd like to say g'day!

I'm a nocturnal Nabarlek, so the nighttime is when I play.

I'm a rock wallaby, like a tiny kangaroo,

and I move with great speed and agility too.

NABARLEK

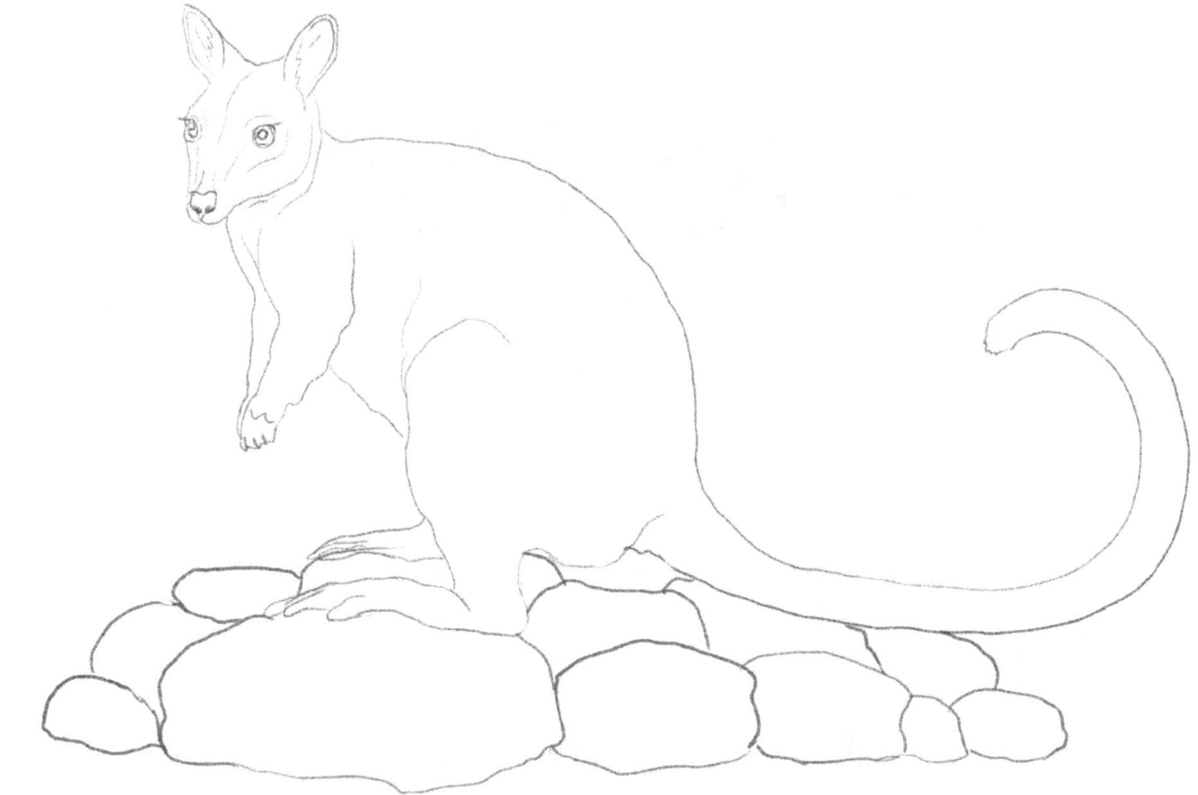

How much fun it would be,
if instead of me, I could be...

An Okapi

(oh-cop-ee)

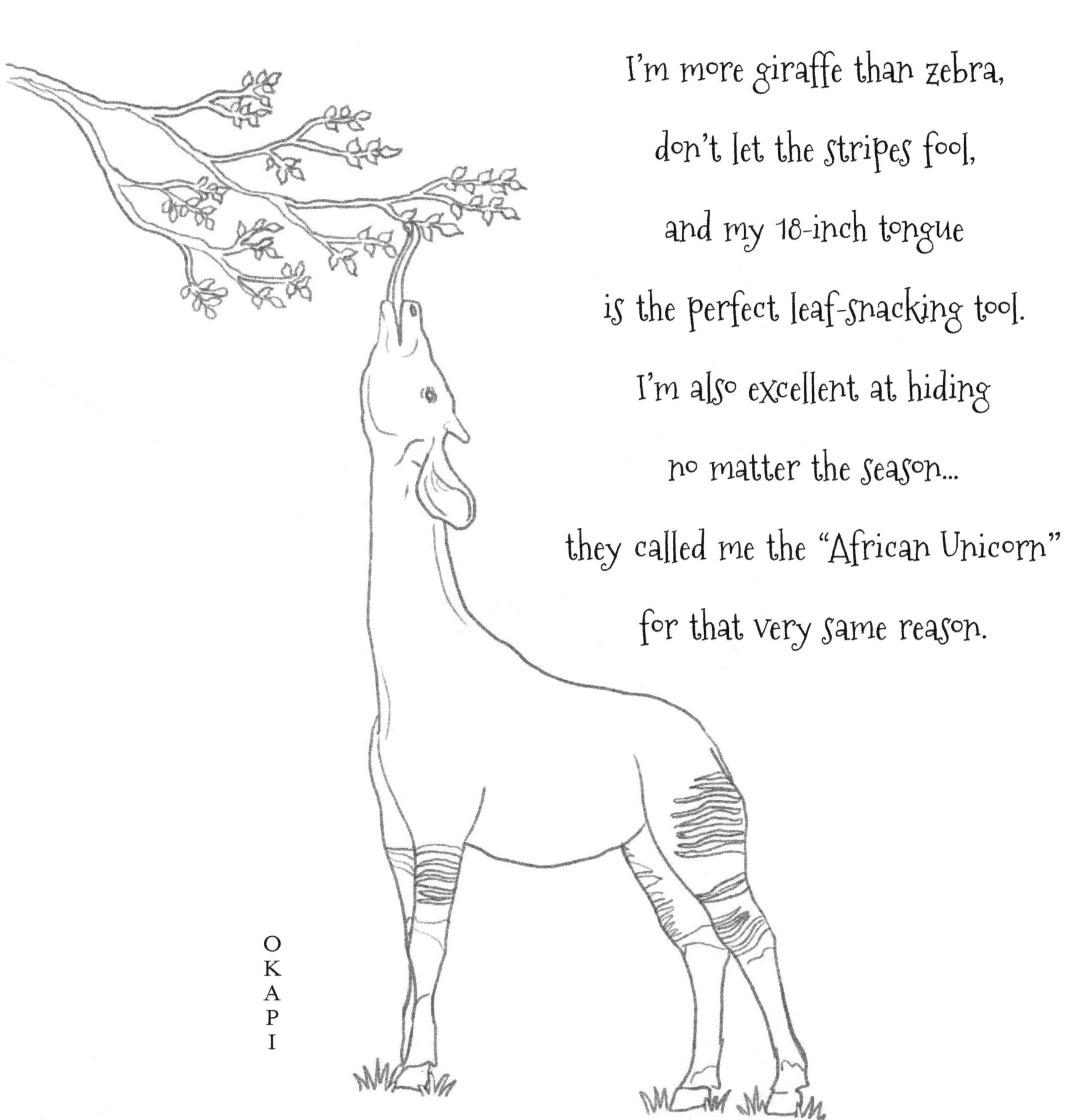

I'm more giraffe than zebra,
don't let the stripes fool,
and my 18-inch tongue
is the perfect leaf-snacking tool.
I'm also excellent at hiding
no matter the season...
they called me the "African Unicorn"
for that very same reason.

OKAPI

How much fun it would be,
if instead of me, I could be...

A Pangolin

(pain-go-lin)

I'm known as the scaly anteater, and I climb and dig like a pro.

The only mammal covered in scales...as a Pangolin, I put on quite the show.

My defense mechanism is super cool, it's like I become an iron wall...

If ever I feel threatened, I curl up in an armor-covered ball.

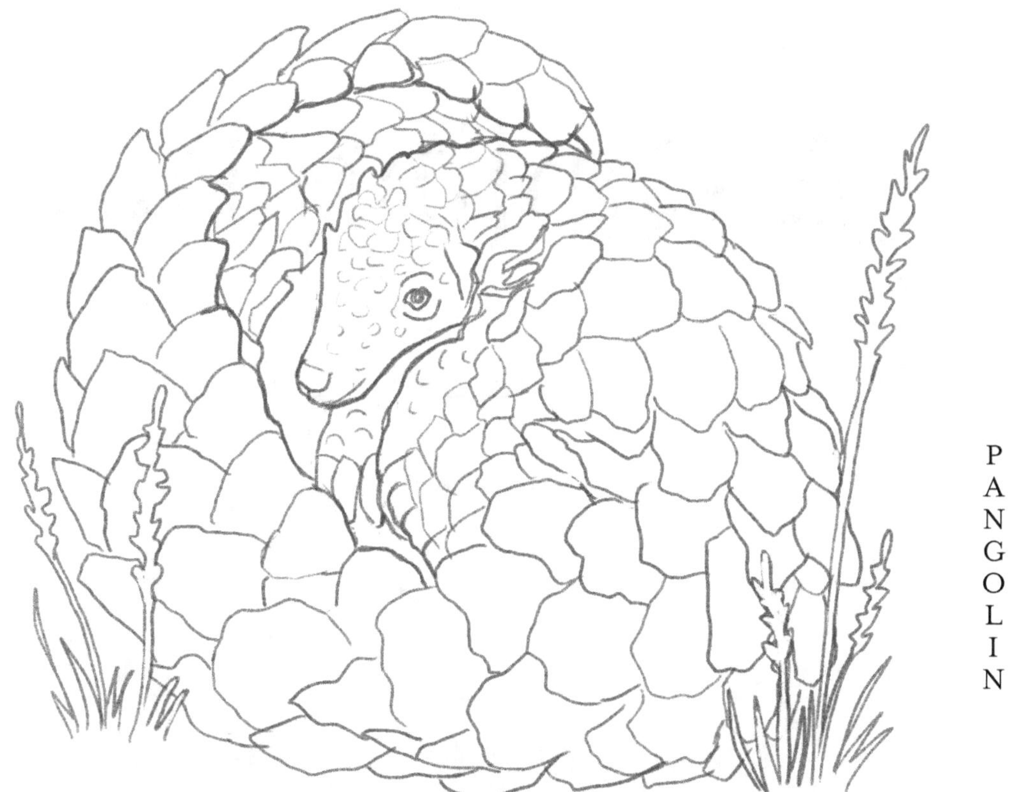

How much fun it would be,
if instead of me, I could be...

A Qinling Panda

(kin-ling pan-duh)

As a rare, giant panda, life isn't always black and white,

because my fur is brown, and quite a unique sight.

In the mountains of China, I love to sleep and eat too.

Which is good, because every day

I eat 40 pounds of bamboo!

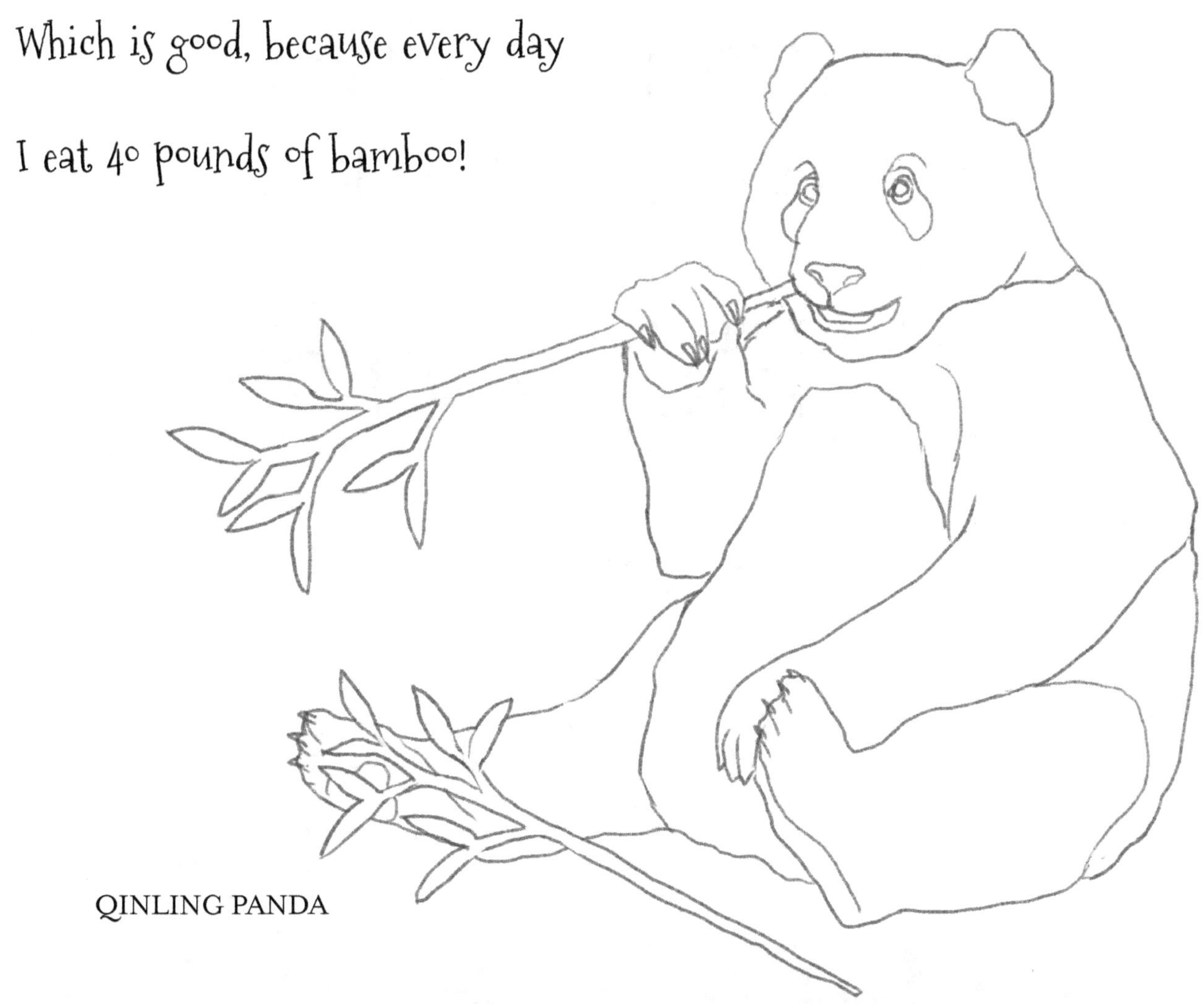

QINLING PANDA

How much fun it would be,
if instead of me, I could be...

A Rhinoceros

(rine-ahh-sir-us)

Africa and Asia are my stomping grounds,
and when I say stomp, I mean it. I weigh 5,000 pounds!
My name means "horn nose", and in the mud, I love to splash,
and when my friends and I get together, our group is called a "crash".

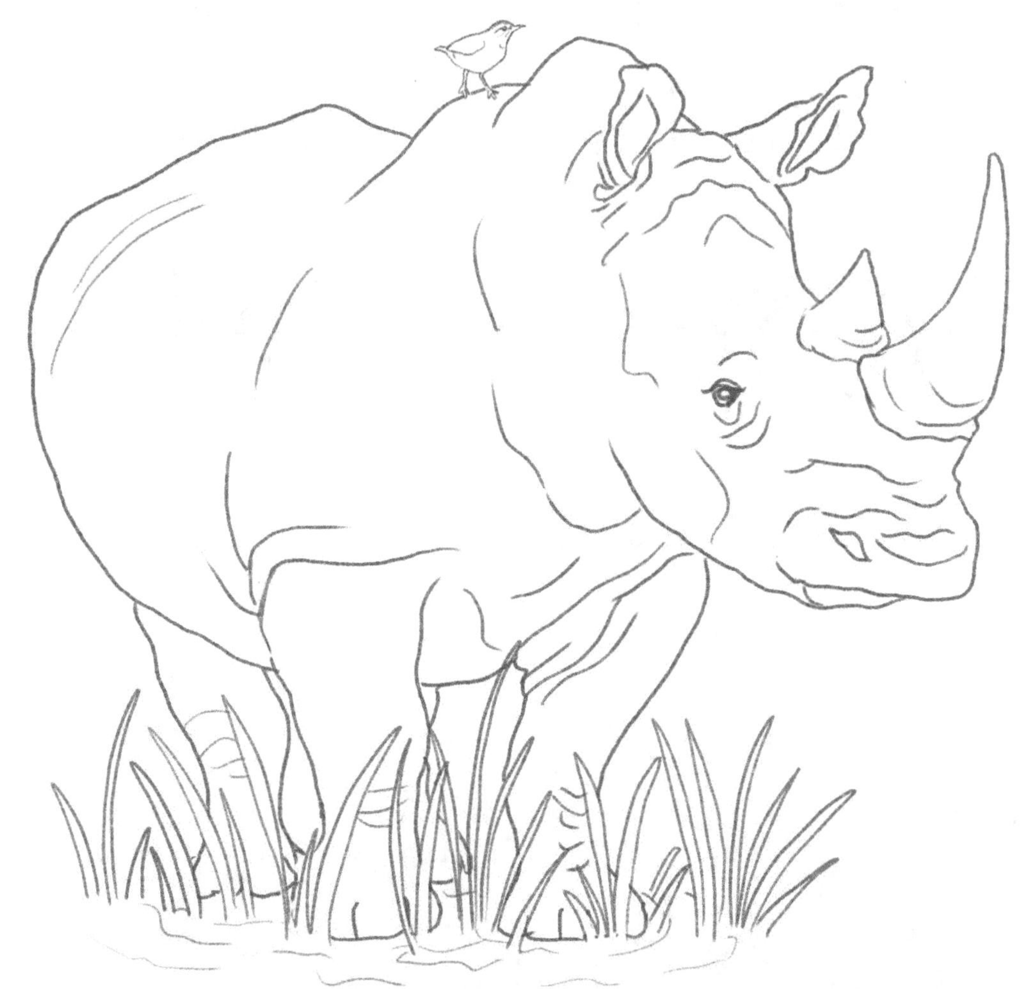

RHINOCEROS

How much fun it would be,
if instead of me, I could be...

A Snowy Owl

(snow-ee ow-wool)

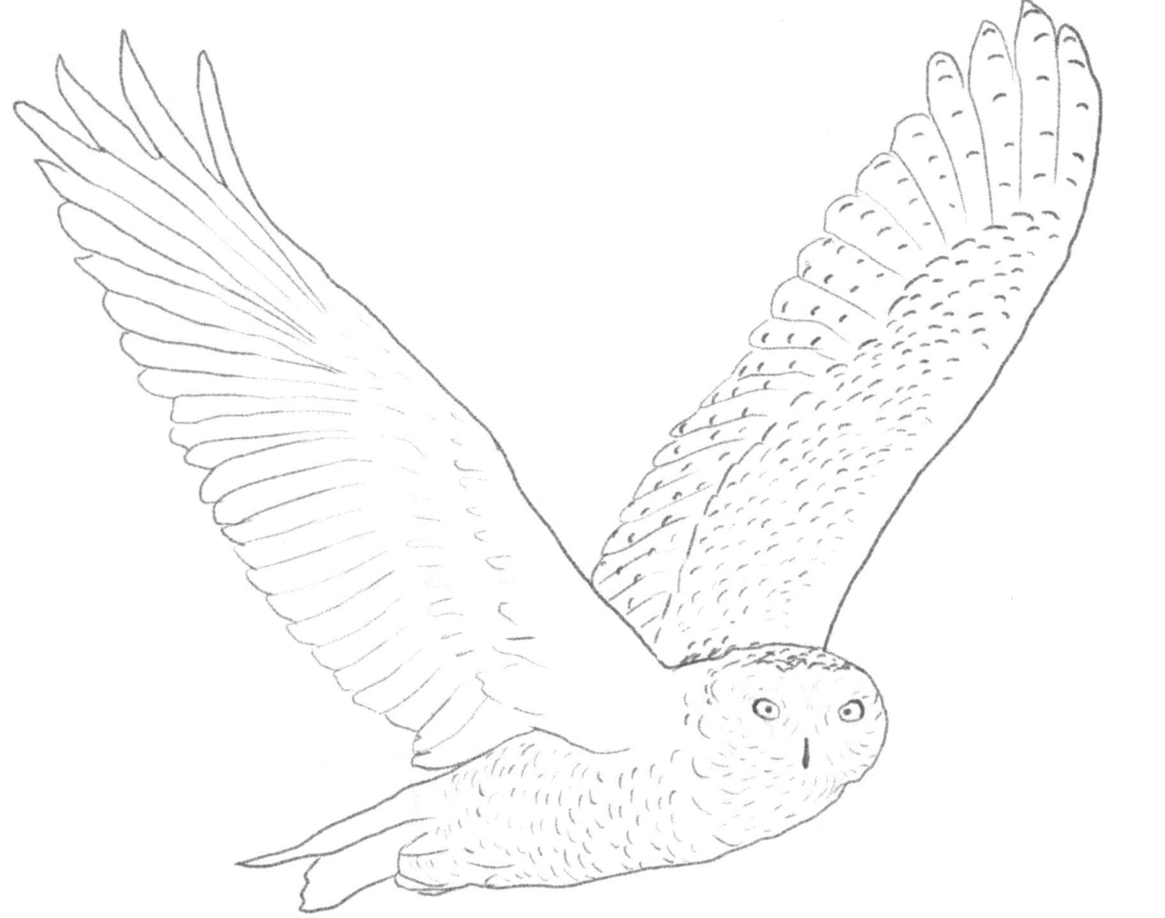

SNOWY OWL

I'm from the arctic tundra, where my feathers are my disguise.

As a majestic Snowy Owl, I have piercing yellow eyes.

I can turn my head to see behind me, and I see and hear like an ace.

With big wings I glide silently, as I fly with stealth and grace.

How much fun it would be,
if instead of me, I could be...

A Tuatara

(too-uh-tar-uh)

My home is New Zealand, on the rocky, island shores,

and my family has been roaming since the age of dinosaurs!

Please don't confuse me with a lizard, there's only one type of me.

I'm so unique, I have a third eye that you can't even see.

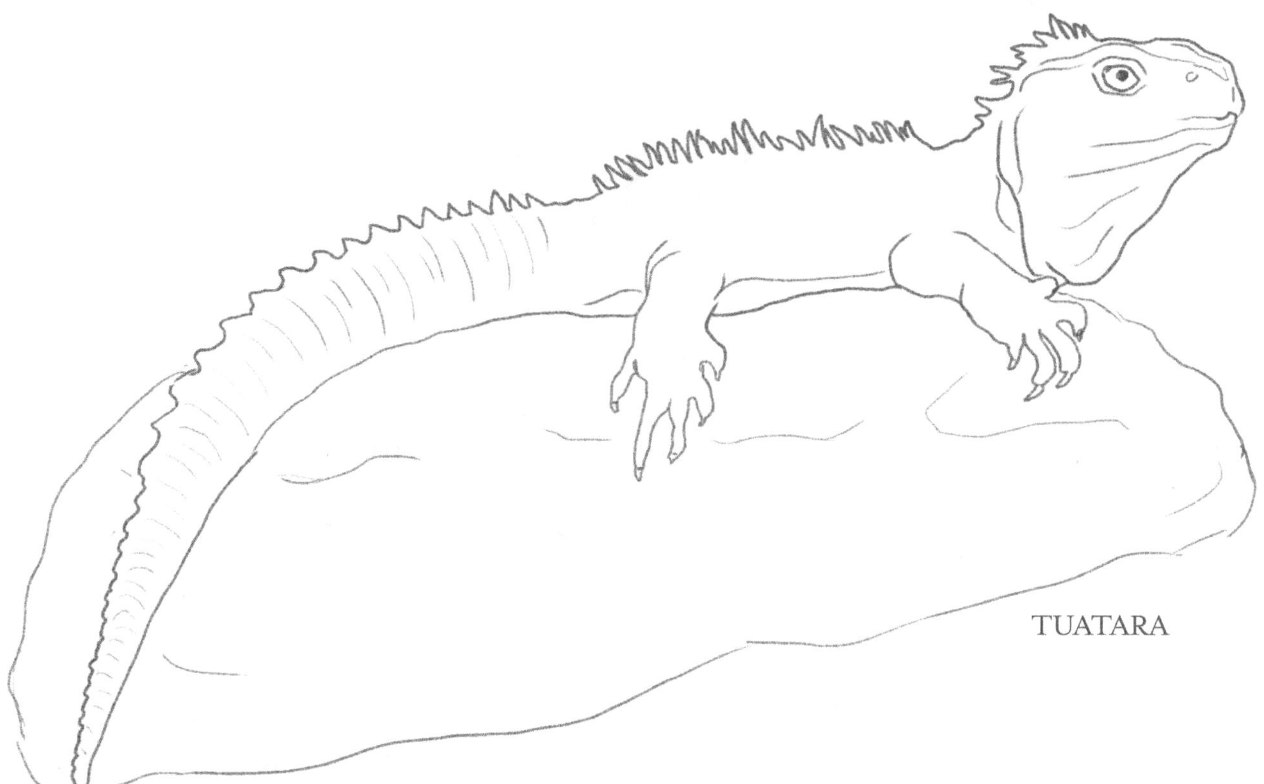

TUATARA

How much fun it would be,
if instead of me, I could be...

A Uakari

(wah-car-ee)

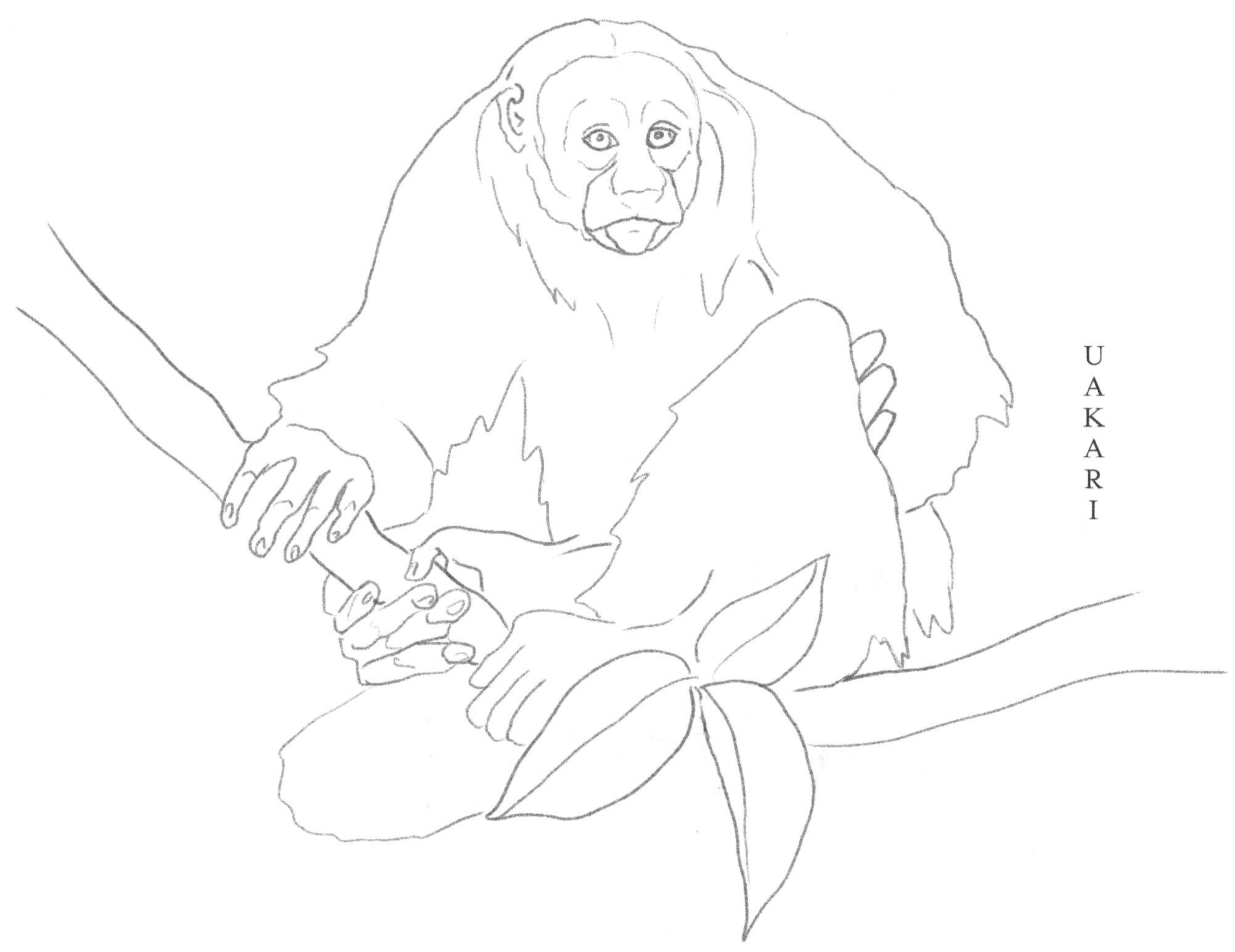

I live in the Amazon Rainforest, where my long hair flows in the breeze.
When the floods come rushing through, no worries! I live high in the trees.
My bright, red face is an indicator that I am healthy and well,
and with my "troop" of family members, life in the jungle is pretty swell.

How much fun it would be,
if instead of me, I could be...

A Vaquita

(vah-keet-uh)

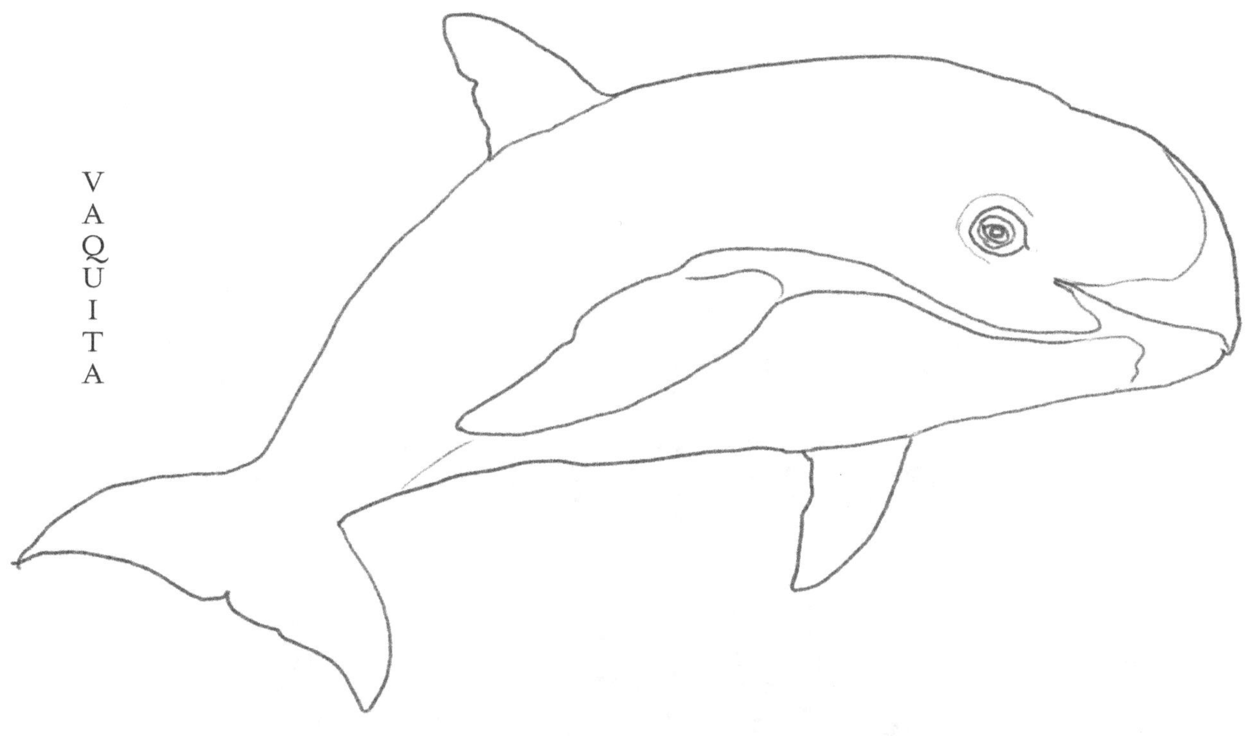

The west coast of Mexico is where I play and swim.

While smaller than my cousin the dolphin, I have a large dorsal fin.

I use sonar, by listening to echoes, to help me find my way.

As the rarest marine mammal in the world, I'm quite unique, wouldn't you say?

How much fun it would be,
if instead of me, I could be...

A Wildebeest

(will-duh-bee-st)

It's not surprising...with a name that means 'Wild Beast',

that I'll roam far around Africa to find the upcoming feast.

Every year, ONE MILLION of us follow the rain as our navigation.

So many walk and munch on fresh grass,

that it's known as The Great Migration.

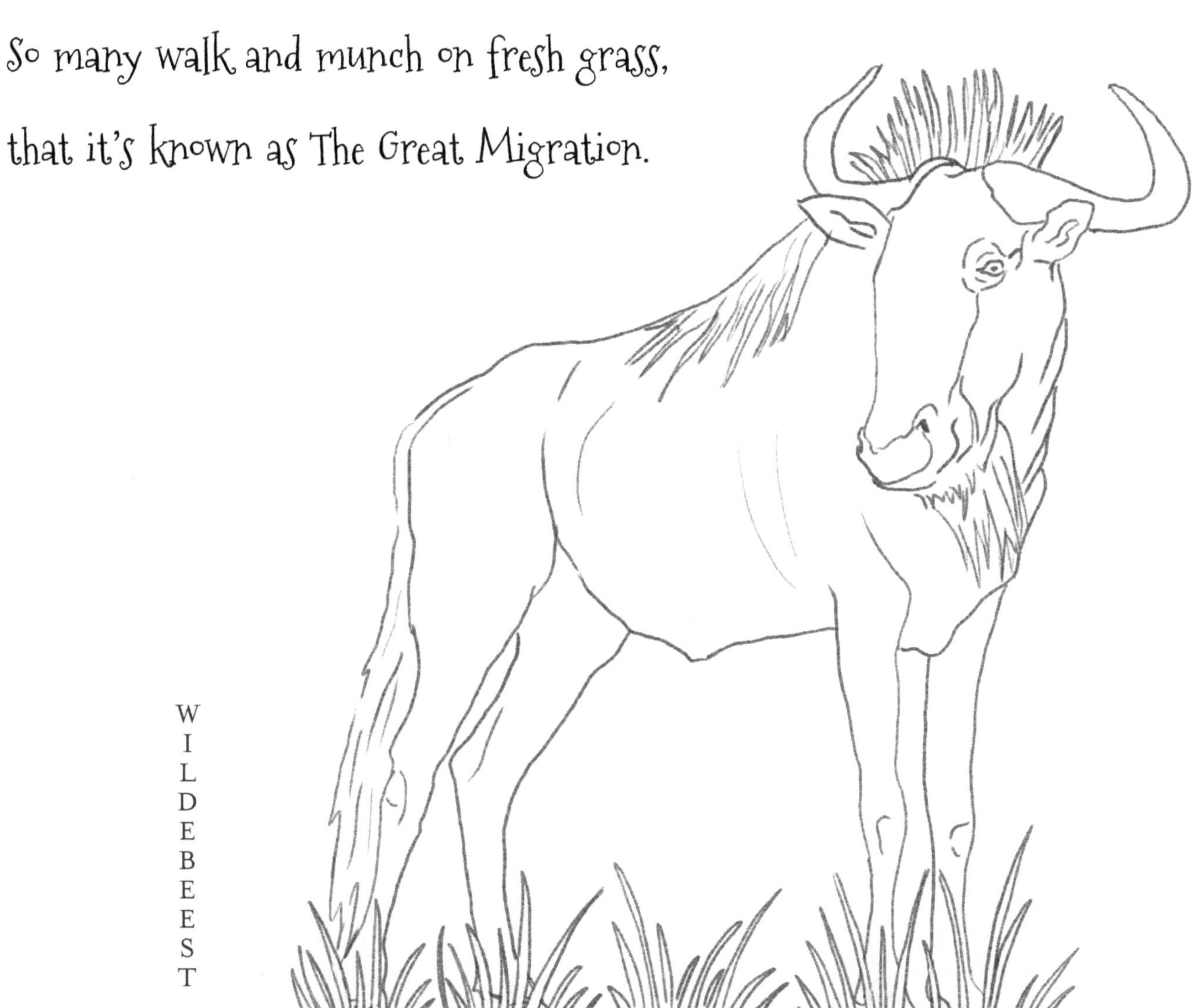

How much fun it would be,
if instead of me, I could be...

A Xenopus

(zee-nuh-puss)

I'm an African frog, and underwater is where I'm found,

I have a lateral line running down my body

that helps me "sense" my way around.

I'm slippery and slick, which helps me move in the water with perfection,

and whether forward, backward, up, or down...

I can swim fast in *any* direction.

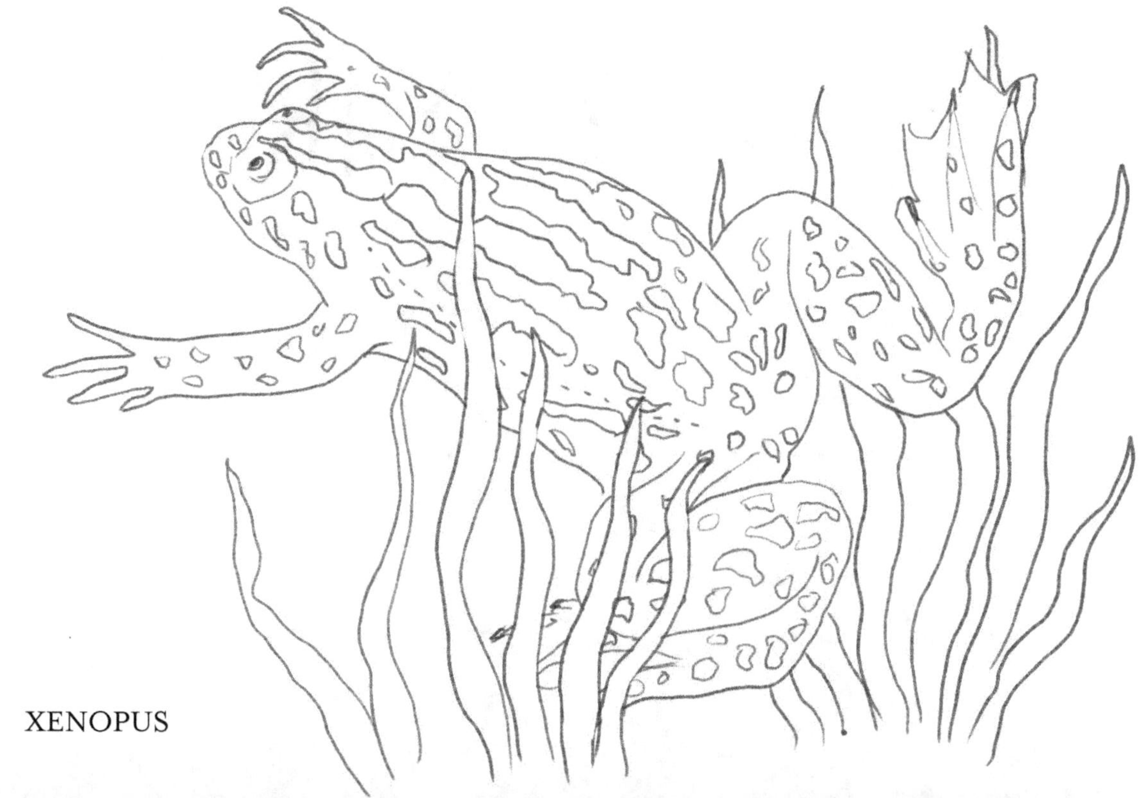

XENOPUS

How much fun it would be,
if instead of me, I could be...

A Yak

(yack)

I live on the tallest mountains in the world...no mammal on earth lives higher.

I enjoy the cold air of the Himalayas, with a warm coat as my wooly attire.

My big lungs help me breathe, and my horns help me find food in the snow.

At 2,000 pounds I'm a powerful force, even if the temperature is 40 below!

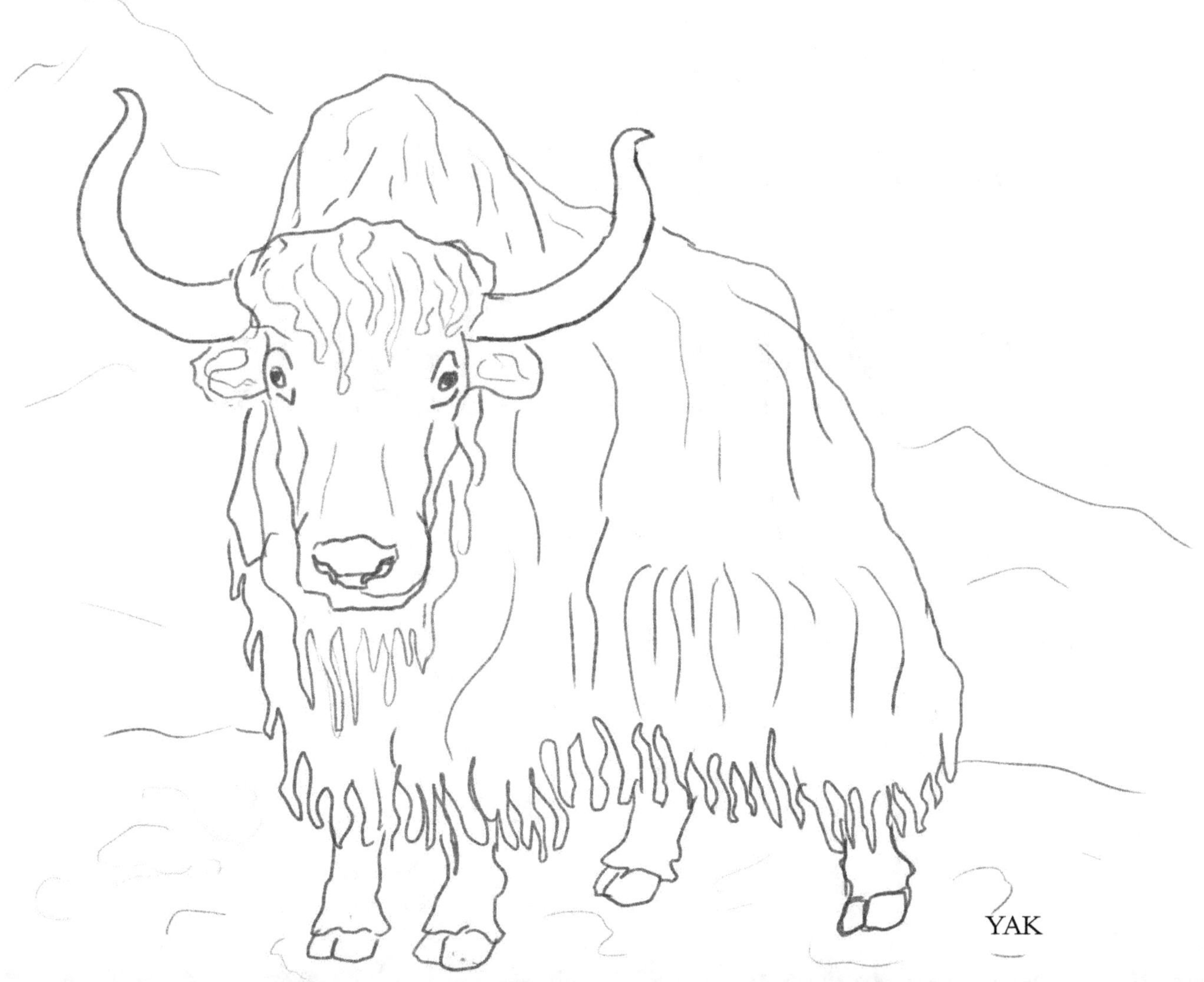

YAK

How much fun it would be,
if instead of me, I could be...

A Zebra Shark

(zee-bruh shar-k)

In Africa, Asia, and Australia, I live in an underwater habitat,

spending my days near the ocean floor, enjoying a reef or a sandy flat.

As a baby, I am designed with stripes and as an adult those change to spots...

So I'm called the Zebra or the Leopard Shark, thanks to my lines and my dots.

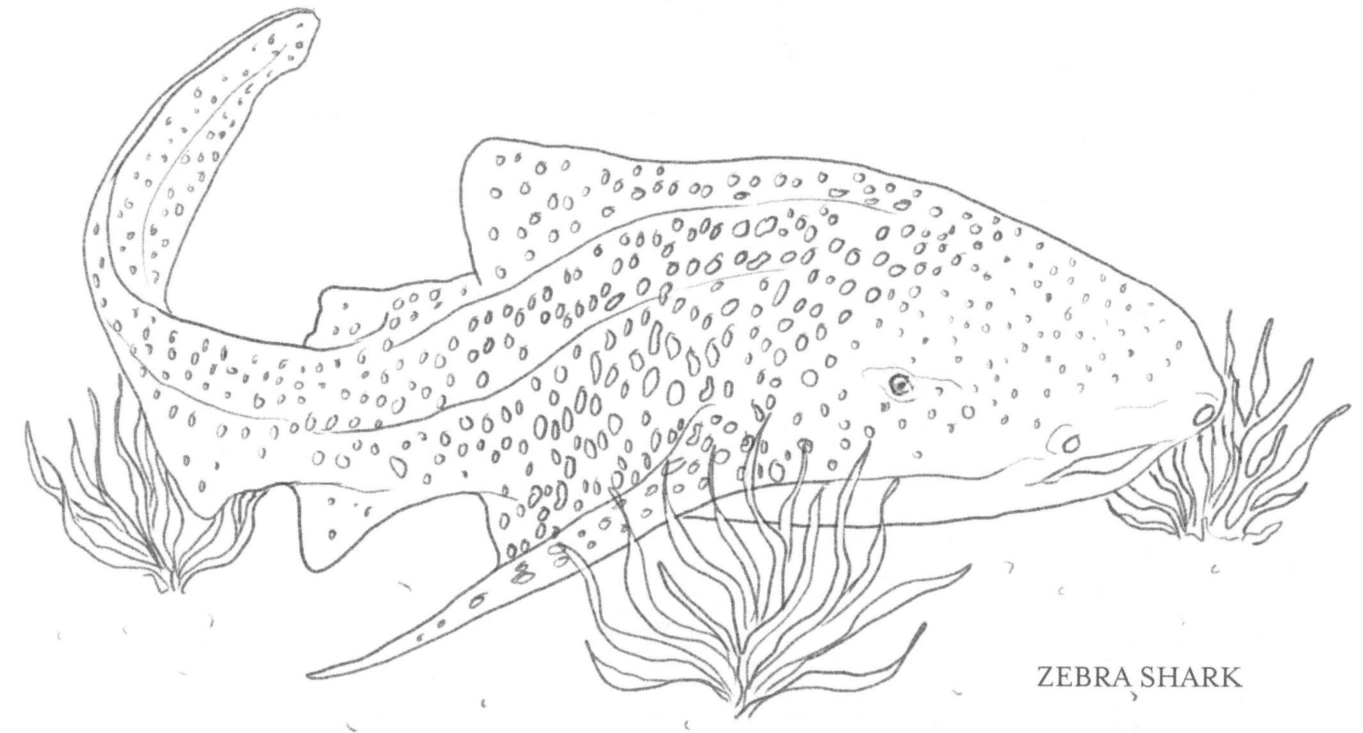
ZEBRA SHARK

Now...

I still lay here in my bed,

and as much as I love those wild animals in my head...

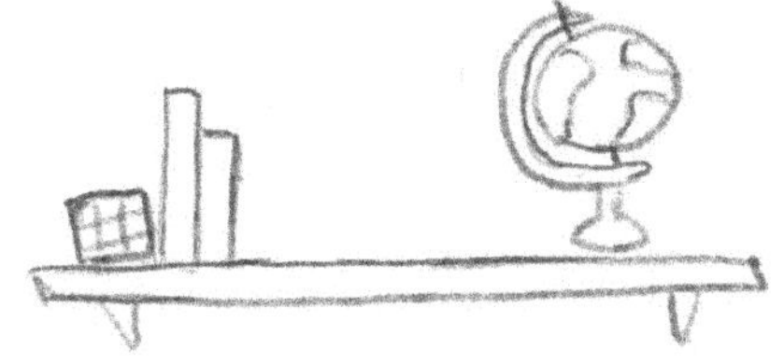

I know that the most fun thing to be,

is the unique and creative human being called ME!

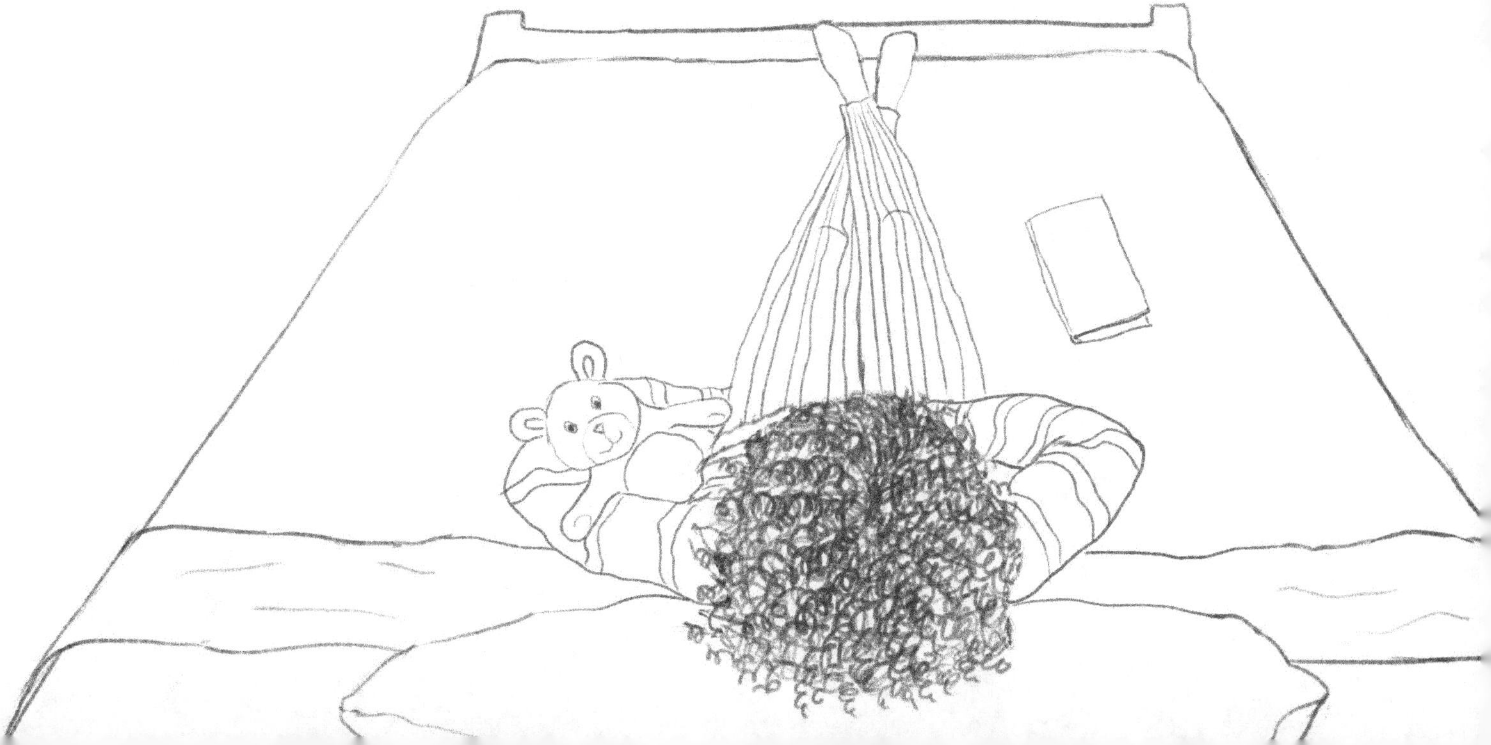

Author

Mike Messeroff

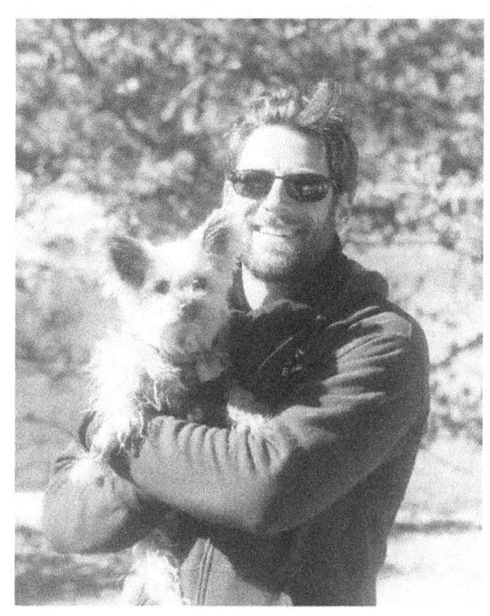

After spending ten years behind a corporate desk in New York City, and several more years as a world-traveling bartender, Mike Messeroff now lives in Breckenridge, Colorado and enjoys the outdoors, travel, and spending time with his wife, friends, his best friend/Yorkshire Terrier "Rocky", and his new puppy "Lela". As Mike began discovering the world of mindfulness and spirituality, he realized that Rocky was naturally exhibiting some of the greatest life skills and habits, and wrote his first book (also with Hannah Chavez), called "Dogs Get It: Advice I learned from my best friend". Mike is also a Personal Freedom Coach, helping others to discover and actualize their greatest desires, and is excited to be sharing his experiences, tips, videos, and new projects on MikeMesseroff.com. Be sure to check it out and join the community!

Illustrator

Hannah Rose Chavez

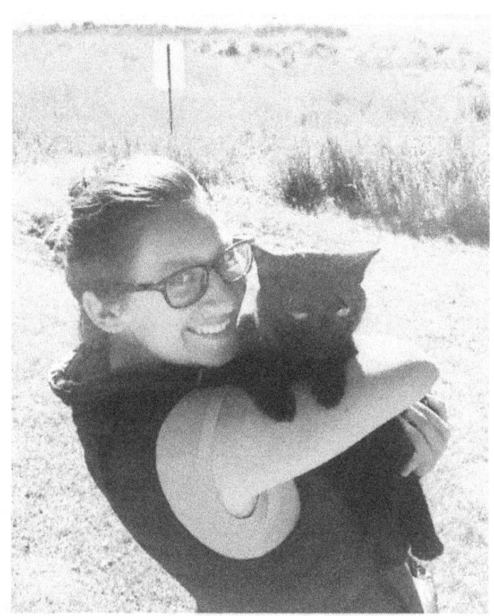

Originally from New York City, Hannah developed a love of art from a young age, along with an understanding of its impact in the world. She spent the last several years in the mountains of Colorado, gaining insights and finding her voice as an artist, and is currently back in New York, focusing on her two main passions: art and animals. She has always felt a deep connection with animals, and is presently accompanied through life by her beloved cat, Mowgli. Working as a freelance artist and illustrator, and using her personal artwork to spread awareness about animal welfare and conservation issues, Hannah has found a way to combine her passions into a purposeful career. A portion of her art profits is also donated to animal rescue organizations. To see more of her work, visit her website at: hannahchavezart.com.

www.ingramcontent.com/pod-product-compliance
Lightning Source LLC
LaVergne TN
LVHW061256100826
845148LV00008B/1144